The End of the Line:

the Newfoundland Railway in Pictures

by
Clayton D. Cook

Harry Cuff Publications Ltd.
St. John's, Newfoundland
1989

Acknowledgements

Appreciation is expressed to the Canada Council for publication assistance.

The publisher acknowledges the financial contribution of the Cultural Affairs Division of the Department of Culture, Recreation and Youth, Government of Newfoundland and Labrador, which has helped make this publication possible.

Canadian Cataloguing in Publication Data

Cook, Clayton D. (Clayton Daniel), 1921-

    The end of the line

    ISBN 0-921191-39-1

1. Newfoundland Railway Company — History — Pictorial works. 2. Railroads — Newfoundland — History — Pictorial works. I. Title.

HE2809.N4C66 1989   385ʹ.065ʹ718   C89-098602-9

Published by
Harry Cuff Publications Ltd.
One Dorset Street
St. John's, Newfoundland
A1B 1W8

Printed in Canada by
ROBINSON-BLACKMORE PRINTING AND PUBLISHING LIMITED
St. John's, Newfoundland

COVER

The front cover, the "Overland Limited" at Wreckhouse, was painted by an artist friend of mine, Willis Hancock. Mr. Hancock painted the Overland in 1983, with myself providing advice, research, planning and formatting. In 1984 Hancock painted a second train, Canadian National's steam passenger train, the "Caribou", again with my assistance. He has since done several other paintings detailing Newfoundland's rich transportation history and will hopefully paint many more.

The back cover is a Hancock portrait of myself in my conductor's uniform.

A NOTE ON PHOTOGRAPHS

The photographs reproduced in this book are the fruit of more than 20 years of collecting and have been made available to me by various sources, including public photo collections, professional photographers and many enthusiastic amateurs. Credits, for the most part, refer to the sources from which I obtained the photos, rather than the photographers (although in some cases the photographer and the source are one and the same).

Every effort has been made to trace copyright owners for these photos to obtain permission to reproduce, and appropriate credit has been given. Uncredited photos are mostly my own, but also include a small number which I could not trace.

I would like to offer particular thanks to the following individuals and organizations which either provided me with railway photographs or assisted me in my collecting.

Ted Bartlett, Marine Atlantic.
Provincial Archives of Newfoundland and Labrador.
Public Archives of Canada.
Canadian Railway Historical Association.
Dr. J.K. Hiller, Memorial University.
Homer Hill.
Karl Purchase.
Gertrude Hynes.
Richard Forest.
Stan Pieda.
Rosalind Power.
R.E. Sparkes, Terra Transport.
The Evening Telegram.
The Western Star.
The Gander Beacon.
Ted Budden, Lewisporte.

Bren Dicks, Corner Brook.
Higdon Photographics.
C. Hoddinott.
Bert Strong, Clarenville.
Gordon Fogwell, Millertown.
Tom Garrett, Terra Nova.
Francis Kelly, Trinity.
Stephen Parsons, Clarenville.
Greg Seaward, Gander.
Jack Sheppard, Glovertown.
Brendan Kenney, St. John's.
Dr. Clayton Hann, Gander.
Gary Callahan, Terra Transport.
Captain J. Prim, Marine Atlantic.
Charlie Butt, Musgravetown.
Albert Burgess, Newfoundland Dockyard.
Ron Walsh, Terra Transport.
James R. Brown.
Irene Pearcey, St. John's.
Mrs. Harvey Guy, Lethbridge.
Silas Avery, Southport.
Baldwin Locomotive Works, Philadelphia, USA.
Alco Historic Photos.
Frances Maidment.
General Motors of Canada Limited.
The Honourable John Crosbie.
Mona Peddle, Lethbridge.
Burwell Barbour.
Sheldon Legrow.
Dr. M. Hadley.
John Over, *The Packet.*
The Quebec North Shore and Labrador Railway.
Gordon King, who provided valuable assistance pertaining to photographic layout.
Omer Lavallee, author of *Narrow Gauge Railways of Canada*. Anyone interested in this, or other books published by Railfare Enterprises, should write for a current catalogue to PO Box 97, Hawkesbury ON, K6A 2R4.

ACKNOWLEDGEMENT

In compiling this work, assistance was forthcoming from many individuals whose interest in seeing the history of our railway preserved was equal to my own. Many of the people listed in the "Note on Photographs" provided encouragement far beyond the mere providing of photographs. I should like to acknowledge their role in this collection once more, as well as the many interested individuals who have encouraged me or prodded me along towards getting this work completed.

I also owe a thank you to my publisher, Harry Cuff. Thanks also to Robert Cuff for his patience and understanding in editing my manuscript.

Finally, I would like to acknowledge a long-standing and very special debt that I owe to my wife, Alice.

DEDICATION

To the memory of my parents, who guided me with affection during my youth.

And to the many fine railwaymen in Newfoundland and across Canada, with whom I was associated during my 33 years with the Newfoundland and Canadian National Railways.

— Clayton D. Cook

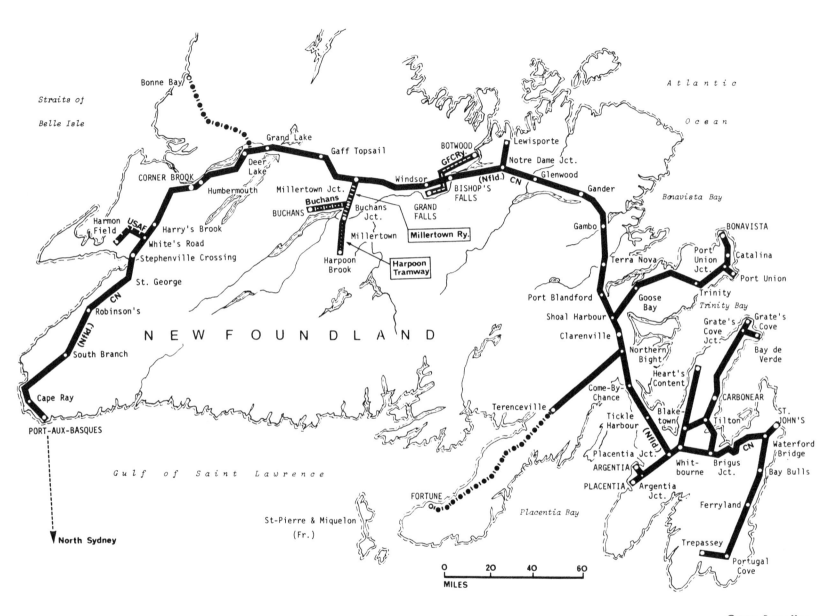

Omer Lavallee

TABLE OF CONTENTS

A WAY OF LIFE

*The Newfie bullet was built on tradition and
very often ran on it. Loyalty to the Company, devo-
tion to duty, resourcefulness, dedication to the task
at hand and ingenuity are inseparable ingredients
of the whole mixture. The Newfie bullet was more
than a transportation link, it was a way of life.*
— Michael Harrington

Although it has a beginning and an end, this is not a complete story. To tell the many untold stories of the Newfoundland Railway would fill more than one book.

I was born into a railway family. From a very early age it was my ambition to work with trains, among the hard-working and versatile railwaymen. I first went to work for the railway at the tender age of fifteen and I witnessed many changes in 33 years railroading, before taking early retirement in 1969. In my retirement I began to research steam passenger trains all over the world, gathering railway photographs and memorabilia, expressing the belief that "someone" should be making a concerted effort to preserve the history of the Newfoundland Railway. Eventually, it occurred to me that perhaps I was that someone and I began collecting in earnest. A selection of photographs from my collection is reproduced herein. It is my fervent hope that, through this book, some future generation of Newfoundlanders will experience some of the joy that the railway gave to us and join me in proudly saying "that was our very own".

C-6369 C.C.&F.CO.LTD. NOV 1943.

CN Photo.

Corner Brook in the 1950s. Departure of the #2 express (eastbound).

A construction gang on the Bonavista branch *c*1910.

A fine crowd turns out to meet a coastal steamer as she arrives in St. John's.

Provincial Archives of Newfoundland and Labrador.

Departing Port aux Basques in the 1940s. The gentleman in the shirtsleeves, right, is station agent Hector Howe. I can never see this photograph without being reminded of trainman Cyril Daniels, a great wit. A passenger once asked him if the train stopped at Port aux Basques. Daniels replied, "Missus, if it doesn't there is going to be one hell of a splash".

CN Photo # X-30881.

Two locomotives of the 2-8-2 Mikado type shortly before they were scrapped in 1957. The numbers refer to the distribution of wheels, an identifying characteristic of steam locomotives. A Mikado engine had two pony wheels in front, eight of the large driving wheels and two trailer truck wheels.

Karl Purchase.

A pair of Mikado 2-8-2 type locomotives (oil burners of the 300 class) head passenger train #2, the ''Caribou'', down Cook's Brook eastbound into Corner Brook. Mid 1950s.

Karl Purchase.

Locomotive #1005 heads a consist of bundled pulpwood for Bowater's mill in Corner Brook, photographed at Main Dam.

CN Photo # X-31306.

The ''Caribou'' eastbound from Port aux Basques, photographed during the mid 1960s.

CN Photo # 67667.

How the mighty have fallen. The Carbonear "mixed" (freight and passengers), one of the last passenger runs. Photographed in 1983.

Homer Hill.

A young boy is entertained by a passenger. For me travel by passenger train has always had a certain momentousness — a separation from ordinary life that travel by motor car or aeroplane cannot hope to match.

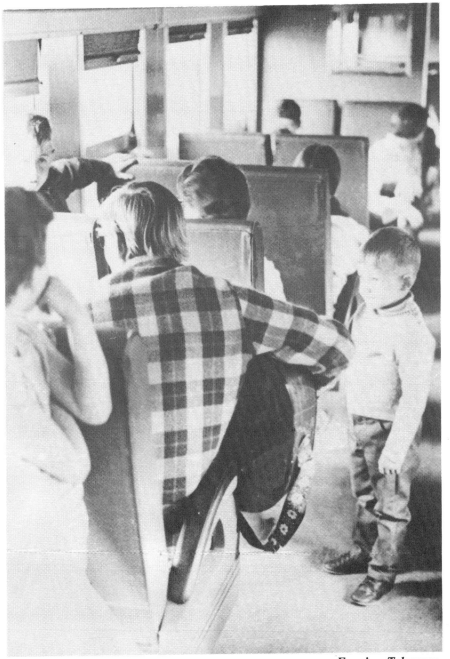

Evening Telegram.

THE WORK OF A COUNTRY

*We do not regard it **per se** as an enterprise that will pay, or as one that offers attractions to speculators, but as the work of a country, and in its bearing on the promotion of the well being of the people, in which the returns are sought and will be found. It eminently commends itself to our judgement.*

— Joint Committee of the House of Assembly and Legislative Council, 1880

Sir William V. Whiteway led his party to victory in the general election of 1878 on a platform that included a promise of action concerning various proposals to build a railway across Newfoundland. Whiteway's first move was to approach the British government for financial assistance for the projected line. The British held that the rail line would be of no strategic or commercial importance to the Empire and would, in fact, cause friction with the French over treaty rights on the west coast. As an alternative Whiteway proposed to the legislature that the government should enter an arrangement with a contractor to build a narrow gauge line from St. John's to Halls Bay, with a branch line to Harbour Grace.

Work began at St. John's on 16 August 1881. By 1884 the line had reached Harbour Grace. There, progress stalled, as the original contractors went into receivership. The government built an additional line to Placentia from Whitbourne in 1886-88 as a public work.

A new contractor, Robert G. Reid, entered the picture in 1890 and contracted to build and equip the line to Halls Bay. The railroad was never to reach Halls Bay, as in 1893 Reid entered into a new contract to construct and operate a line which would extend to Port aux Basques. The final link of the Newfoundland Northern and Western Railway was completed in 1898.

Omer Lavallee.

The first locomotives of the Newfoundland railway were purchased from the Prince Edward Island Railroad in 1881 and arrived in St. John's on 5 December of that year aboard the S.S. *Merlin*. The locomotives were of the Hunslett 4-4-0 type and were built in 1872. None were still in use in 1897.

Locomotive #8 was one of the first built expressly for the Newfoundland Railway. A 2-6-0 tender type, built by Hawthorne Leslie of Leeds in 1882 it was renumbered 21 in 1898 and was scrapped in the early 1900s.

Baldwin Locomotive Works.

Engine #4 was built for the Halls Bay Railroad by Baldwin Locomotive Works of Philadelphia in 1891. A 2-6-0 tender type, it was renumbered 60 in 1898 and scrapped in the early 1900s.

The original station and freight depot at Fort William in St. John's (near the present-day site of the New-foundland Hotel). The station was destroyed in a fire 31 March 1900.

Sir Robert Gillespie Reid (1842-1908). Reid was born in Scotland and worked extensively in railroad contracting in Australia, the United States and Canada before undertaking the building of the railway from Whitbourne to Halls Bay in 1890. In 1893 he contracted to continue the line to Port aux Basques and to operate the railroad for 10 years.

After construction was completed in 1898, Reid undertook to operate the railroad for 50 years. The Reid Newfoundland Company also took over the coastal boat services and the St. John's dockyard under the terms of the famous Railway Contract of 1898.

CN Photo.

A mixed train on the run to Harbour Grace, photographed at Manuels Bridge *c*1885. The locomotive is #9, a 2-6-0 tender type built in 1882 by Hawthorne Leslie of Leeds. It was renumbered 22 in 1898 by the Reid Newfoundland Company and was scrapped in the early 1900s.

A wreck in the late 1890s. Engine #7 was returning from Harbour Grace with salt fish when her boiler blew up, killing engineer Glascow and fireman Byrne.

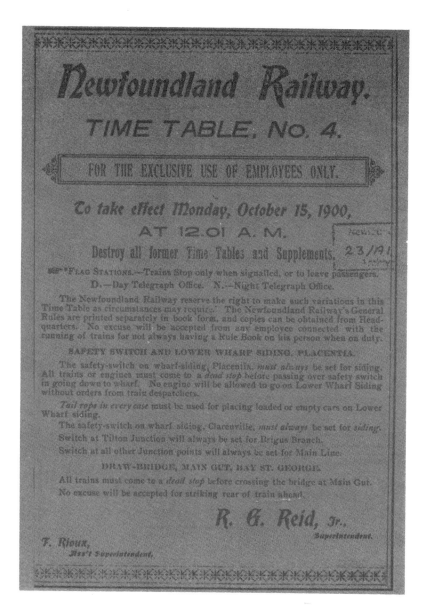

Provincial Archives of Newfoundland and Labrador.

The cover of the Newfoundland Railway timetable for 1900.

Engine #9 was a 2-6-0 tender type, built for the Newfoundland Railway in 1882 by Hawthorne Leslie of Leeds. It would appear that this engine was the pride of the railway in its earliest days, as #9 appears in photographs of many ceremonial occasions.

Sectionmen operating a pump car near Shellbird Island on the Humber River in the early 1900s.

The *Bruce* meets one of the first passenger trains at the terminal in Port aux Basques. The train is made up of three passenger cars, a 2-6-0 type locomotive (#11?) and one combination mail and baggage car.

CN Photo.

LOCOMOTIVES

Every improvement in the means of locomotion benefits mankind morally and intellectually as well as materially.

— T.B. Macaulay

The most vivid of my early memories is of standing at Princeton station, where my father was station master, watching the Bonavista mixed disembark. When the engineer opened the throttle the locomotive spun its wheels in short bursts until it finally got the impossible mass of freight and passengers rolling. Since that time I have not experienced anything to match the magnificence of a steam locomotive, nothing that could convey that same feeling of sheer power. Man's technology has produced many wonders, but nothing that can capture the imagination like the trains of my youth.

It was during my own career as a railwayman that the steam era came to an end. The Newfoundland Railway began to experiment with diesels in the 1940s. By the late 1950s the changeover to diesel power was in full swing. Any railwayman could see the advantages: better mileage out of fuel, the ability to haul heavier cargos and especially the capacity of diesel locomotives to rack up service mileage without requiring the frequent overhauls typical of the age of steam and coal. Yet, those of us who experienced the changeover were all touched by sadness, seeing one classic engine after another broken up for scrap.

Provincial Archives of Newfoundland and Labrador.

A new locomotive out for a test run to Bowring Park. A 4-4-0 tender type, #3 was built in 1891 for the Halls Bay Railroad by the Baldwin Locomotive Works in Philadelphia. It was renumbered 41 in 1898 by the Reid Newfoundland Company and was scrapped in the early 1920s.

Halls Bay Railroad #5 on a fishing expedition at "Jack Burke's", near Harry's River in 1897. Built at the Baldwin Works, this engine was renumbered 42 by Reid's and was scrapped in 1916.

Locomotive #113 was one of ten of the "100-class" built by the Reid Newfoundland Company shops at St. John's. These 4-6-0 type engines were used primarily on the branch lines. This particular engine was scrapped in 1951. The engineer pictured is Andrew Seaward of Clarenville.

Public Archives of Canada # C-26075, Omer Lavallee collection.

Reid's also built two 150-class engines at St. John's in 1916, which were somewhat slow, but had an extra set of driving wheels (2-8-0 consolidated type) and were used primarily for freight. Renumbered 280, this engine was the only one not converted from coal to oil. It spent its last few years switching at Port aux Basques and was scrapped in 1955.

In 1920 six 190-class 4-6-2 type ''Pacific'' engines were purchased from the Baldwin Works. In my day these locomotives were used for branch line service and switching. The engineer pictured is Walter Maidment.

A builder's photograph of #193. This engine was renumbered 593 by CN in 1949. In 1957, when the other 190-class engines were scrapped, #593 was donated to the Corner Brook Rotary Club and it is now at Humbermouth.

In 1929 #198 was built by the American Locomotive Works in Schenectady, NY. A Pacific 4-6-2 type, it was the pride of the Newfoundland Railway and was used for the passenger service until the arrival of the 1000-class, when it was relegated to mainline freight. It was sold to the Botwood Railway in 1957 and was scrapped the following year.

This is #1000, first of the 2-8-2 type 1000-class "Mikado" engines. Built for the heavy grades of the New-foundland Railway by the American Locomotive Works in 1930, #1000 burned half the coal of the 100-class and 150-class. It is pictured shortly before being scrapped in 1957, with its post-Confederation number 300.

Karl Purchase.

Built by the North British Locomotive Company of Glasgow, #1006 was renumbered 306 by CN. It was scrapped in 1957.

Montreal Locomotive Works, Public Archives of Canada #C-26092.

Built in 1947, #1021 was the second locomotive built to be fired by oil and was not a coal-burning conversion. Renumbered 321 by CN, it was scrapped in 1957, after less than 10 years of service.

CN Photo.

One of the last steam locomotives built for the Newfoundland Railway. The Montreal Locomotive Company built #1024 in 1949. This locomotive became part of the consist of the flagship passenger train "Overland Limited". It was renumbered 324 by CN and was scrapped in 1957.

One of three small diesel-electric 380 horsepower locomotives purchased in the late 1940s, the Newfoundland Railway's first taste of the diesel revolution to come. Built by G.E. of Erie, Pennsylvania, these engines were originally the 5000-class, renumbered as 775-777 by CN, and sold to Costa Rica in the late 1960s.

CN Photo # X-38904.

General Motors of Canada Ltd.

One of the 1200 horsepower diesels purchased in 1956 to replace the Newfoundland Railway steam locomotives, built by GM Diesel Division of London, Ontario.

A Terra Transport freight hauled by a pair of 1200 horsepower diesels, passing through Bowring Park. The dieselization program was initiated in 1952 and by 1960 fifty-three diesels were purchased: forty-seven 1200hp ''900 class'' and six 875hp ''800 class''.

CN Photo.

The heaviest headend power ever to operate on the Newfoundland railway. Fourteen locomotives being transferred 'from Clarenville to St. John's for the closing of the railway in September of 1988.

ROLLING STOCK AND OTHER EQUIPMENT

The railway is very substantially constructed and
very efficiently operated: the roadbed is splendidly
built; the rails are the best procurable; the bridges
are of steel with granite abutments, and the rolling
stock is the finest that is made.
— P.T. McGrath, *Newfoundland in 1911*

Although it may have been "the world's slowest crack passenger train", the "Newfie Bullet" was not without its charms. There was a special elegance to lunch as it was served in a dining car. The heavy silver and the excellent food and service all added to the sense of occasion.

During the war years (especially before the arrival of lend-lease equipment) much of the Newfoundland Railway's rolling stock was outdated and in a shocking state of disrepair. Breakdowns were frequent, necessitating temporary repairs on the road, in order to get to one of the division repair depots at Clarenville, Bishop's Falls, Humbermouth or Port aux Basques. Such repairs would often be made by the conductor, as when a stop would be made the trainman would have to walk back to flag any following train.

The station was one of the natural centres of every community touched by the train. This was especially the case in the railway towns like Bishop's Falls, Whitbourne, Clarenville and Port aux Basques.

The water tower and coaling shed at Clarenville in the early 1930s. The locomotive being coaled is one of the 100-class, 4-6-0 type.

A section crew surrounds their track motor car near Lethbridge in the 1940s. The crew consists of Les Smart, Edmund Harris, Ralph Hart (foreman), Frank Smart and Robert Pye.

Steam rotary plow #2, built in 1909 by the American Locomotive Works. The steam rotaries were virtually the only plows capable of dealing with wet deep snow and were often pressed into service on the Gaff Topsails. One rotary, #3, was built by the Reids in St. John's.

The first of the steel push plows, purchased in the late 1940s from Canadian Car and Foundry Company.

One of five self-propelled steam rail cars (or "Day Coaches") built in Britain by Sentinel Cammell between 1923 and 1925. The Day Coaches ran between Humbermouth and Curling West, St. John's and Topsail and were also used for passenger traffic on the branch lines. They were scrapped in the late 1930s after the closure of the Bay de Verde, Heart's Content and Trepassey branches.

Loading first class passenger cars for the Newfoundland Railway at Montreal in October of 1943. The ship is the S.S. *Livingston*, a Bowater's pulp and paper carrier. The cars were unloaded at Corner Brook, where they had their running gear assembled, then hauled to St. John's.

CN Photo.

CN Photo # 67058-6.

The sleeping car *Fogo*, built by Canadian Car and Foundry in Montreal in 1943. The *Fogo* was used primarily on the rear of passenger trains — note the observation platform. It is now a part of the Newfoundland Transport Historical Society's exhibit in St. John's.

Terra Transport.

The interior of the observation car *Bristol*. This car, renamed the *Avalon*, was part of the Overland Limited's consist in the late 1930s and early 1940s.

Canadian Railway History Association, Toohey collection.

The business car *Terra Nova*, used to convey Governor Walwyn to Argentia for the meetings between Roosevelt and Churchill which culminated in the Atlantic Charter. The *Terra Nova* is preserved in the National Museum of Science and Technology in Ottawa.

A standard CN boxcar on 42'' trucks, dwarfing a 30-ton Newfoundland railway boxcar. Converting standard gauge boxcars for use in Newfoundland was a standard practice after Confederation.

The shape of things to come. An eastbound freight transports motor cars through the Humber Valley.

Awaiting the arrival of the regular passenger train at St. George's station in the early 1900s. This station was destroyed by fire in the 1930s.

Bishop's Falls station, sometime in the mid 1960s. For many years Bishop's Falls was the headquarters of the western division.

THE COASTAL BOATS

Today is a red letter day in our annals, the arrival of the Bruce *marks an epoch in Newfoundland history. We are no longer isolated. This magnificent ship. . .is the link that will bind us to the continent, bring us into closer connection with the civilization and superior advancement of America. Up to the present we have lain outside of strong currents of progress, remote, unbefriended and practically unknown, the helpless victim.*
    — Judge D.W. Prowse, *Telegram* 13 Oct 1897

The operation of the coastal steamer service and the Gulf crossing was assumed by the Reid Newfoundland Company in 1898, when the Reids contracted to operate the railway. The previous year Reid had purchased the *Bruce* to link the terminal at Port aux Basques with North Sydney. After signing the railway contract Reid immediately ordered additional steamers for the coastal service from A. & J. Inglis of Glasgow. These ships, which came to be known as the "Alphabet Fleet", included the *Argyle*, *Bruce*, *Clyde*, *Dundee*, *Ethie*, *Fife*, *Glencoe*, and *Home*. Later the *Invermore*, *Kyle*, *Lintrose* and *Meigle* were added.

When the Reids sold the railway to the Newfoundland Government in 1923 the coastal and gulf boats were also sold and continued to be operated by the railway until the operations were turned over to Canadian National in 1949. As a symbol of the new era the *Caribou* was ordered constructed for the gulf crossing — a worthy successor to the *Bruce*.

In 1924 the government acquired the Crosbies' and Bowrings' coastal boats, which had previously operated under a government subsidy. Subsequent additions to the coastal fleet included the *Northern Ranger* in 1936.

The second *Bruce* on her maiden voyage in 1912. The first steamer of that name was lost near Louisbourg in 1911. The second *Bruce* was on the Gulf run for only three years before being sold to the Russian government during World War I.

CN Marine # 73160-2.

The *Glencoe* was the second steamer built by Inglis for Reid's (after the original *Bruce*). It is pictured here at the gantry on the Lewisporte railway dock during the 1940s, being bunkered with coal.

Public Archives of Canada # C-65068, Notman's Photo Series.

The *Clyde* served the ports of Notre Dame Bay for many years, sailing out of Lewisporte. She was sold to Crosbie and Company in 1948 and was lost near Williamsport on 17 December 1951.

Captain J. Prim.

The *Dundee* was built by A. & J. Inglis in 1900. For many years she was on the Bonavista Bay run. The *Dundee* would leave Port Blandford every Monday after the arrival of the #1 and #2 passenger trains with mail, passengers and general cargo for the Bonavista Bay ports.

B. Kenney.

The *Ethie* at the Newfoundland Dockyard. She was built by A. & J. Inglis in 1900 and was lost at Martin Point, St. Barbe, 11 December 1919.

The *Kyle* was built for the Reid Newfoundland Company in 1913 by Swan Hunter & Company of Newcastle. She was built primarily for the Labrador service, but was also used for the Cabot Strait crossing for a number of years. The *Kyle* was sold in 1959 and ran aground at Harbour Grace in 1962. She has been lying derelict there ever since.

Captain J. Prim.

The *Portia*, pictured, and her sister ship, the *Prospero*, were built for Bowring Brothers in 1904 by Murdoch & Murray of Glasgow. For 20 years Bowrings operated the ships in the coastal service with the aid of a subsidy. They were purchased by the Newfoundland government in 1924 along with Crosbies' *Sagona* and *Fogota*.

The *Caribou* arriving in St. John's 22 October 1925 on her maiden voyage, after being built in Rotterdam by the firm of A. Goodwin, Hamilton Adamson. After several years on the Gulf crossing she was sunk by enemy action on 14 October 1942.

The S.S. *Burgeo*, built by Fleming & Ferguson of Paisley, Scotland in 1940 for the coastal service, along with her sister ship the *Baccalieu*.

Charlie Butt.

In 1946 the government ordered three more ships from Fleming and Ferguson: the *Bar Haven*, the *Springdale* and the *Cabot Strait*. The *Cabot Strait* is pictured here having run aground near Cape Ray on 17 January 1957. She was retired in 1974.

The *Burin*, one of ten wooden steamers built at Clarenville in the 1940s. Another of the "Splinter Fleet", the *Trepassey*, can be seen at left.

The *William Carson* was the first of the ice-breaking auto ferries, built for the Gulf run in 1955 by Canadian Vickers of Montreal. The *Carson* was lost off Square Island 2 June 1977, shortly after being reassigned to the Labrador run.

CN Photo # 51259-1.

Sheldon Legrow.

The second *Caribou*, at her launch party in St. John's on 28 May 1986, shortly after her maiden voyage.

THE RAILWAYMEN

From the day that I entered the employ of the railway I did not have a dull moment. There, work was different every day, always challenging and offering good opportunities to meet people.
— W.J. Chafe, *I've Been Working on the Railroad*

There was a fascination about railroading that hard work and low pay could not diminish. The trainman's life was never dull and in the midst of the serious business of running a railroad the employees always had the spirit to appreciate the pleasures of railroading. My co-workers had a warmth, humour and vitality that I have seldom seen matched. When this was coupled with the loyalty that the railwaymen had to each other it is easy to see why the job held such charm for me.

However, railroading in Newfoundland could also be dangerous and uncomfortable in the extreme. Many of my valued co-workers were seriously injured or killed in train wrecks. There was also the unwritten law of the railway that operating crews should make every effort to complete their runs, no matter how long it took. Crews could be on the road for several days without rest or adequate food. This seemed to happen several times every winter in the Gaff Topsails area, where crews were occasionally stuck for weeks at a time.

Stephen Parsons.

A construction gang at work on the Bonavista branch in 1910.

Dr. Clayton Hann.

A pile driving crew, employed by the railway to build temporary wooden bridges, when structures were carried away by flooding or river ice. They also built railway wharves and did a variety of other piling work. The gentleman in the foreground is Douglas Hann of Port aux Basques. Others include members of the Ford family of Port Blandford.

Stephen Parsons.

A railway telegrapher at work. Pictured is George Nicholls at Shoal Harbour in the early 1920s.

A steam shovel crew at Shoal Harbour pit in 1936. The large steam shovels usually required two ballast trains to keep them operating, one running east, the other west. Pictured are the engineers, the conductor, the ballast crews, shovel operator and the cook car crew.

CN Photo.

Irene Pearcey.

General manager of the Newfoundland Railway, H.J. Russell, and assistant general manager J.V. Ryan.

Gordon King.

Striking railway workers. Men from the different branches gathered at St. John's to back up their wage demands in the 1940s. Working conditions had been particularly dangerous during the War years as men and trains had been pushed to the limit of their capacities in the name of the war effort. Small wonder that railwaymen were determined to get a better wage by the time the war ended. The strike lasted for a month and achieved a $10 per month increase across the board.

Richard Forest.

Trainman Job Blackmore and his wife enjoy a light lunch during the last run of the Carbonear mixed train,
20 September 1984.

The train crew who operated the last passenger carrying train from Bishop's Falls to Corner Brook 2 October 1988. Crew L-R: engineer Pierce Farrell, conductor Carl Dillon, trainman Patrick O'Reilly, trainman William Penney and trainman Stan Pieda.

In working on the Newfoundland Railway there were often unpleasant jobs that simply had to be done. Here workmen Reg Roach and Robert Bailey break the track at mileage 340 on the Gaff Topsails 12 October 1988.

Stan Pieda.

WRECKS AND DERAILMENTS

In life and death the engineer
His duty well he knew,
He had just reversed his engine
To save his train and crew.
They held their post so bravely
In the wreckage where they lay
It seemed as when they saw the end
Both calmly looked away.
— Gilbert Lynch
"The Wreck of Train Number 32"

Unfortunately, wrecks were a large part of the railwayman's life. There were "everyday" dangers that demanded constant vigilance against derailments: snow conditions, spread rails, sun-kinks (when the rails were expanded by the heat of the sun), moose on the tracks and curves thrown out of alignment. Every railwayman took these dangers in stride and tried to lessen their damage by constant awareness, respect for their equipment and being prepared to cope with emergencies as they arose.

There were also numerous tragic level crossing accidents involving vehicles or pedestrians and there is one particular occasion etched upon my memory when two young boys attempting to hitch a ride had their legs severed. By far the most horrendous "regular" occurrences, however, were the many collisions that occurred. It was not unusual for a railwayman, in the course of a career on the Newfoundland Railway, to have seen several treasured comrades lose their lives. I was personally involved in two collisions: a rear-end collision at Cooks Brook where there was no serious injury and a head-on collision at Crow Head which resulted in several serious injuries and three deaths.

Provincial Archives of Newfoundland and Labrador. Sir Leonard Outerbridge Collection.

An accident caused by a cow on the tracks *c*1901 on the old main line to the Fort William terminal, just
before it crossed Kingsbridge Road. Engine #60 was the former Halls Bay Railroad #4.

Bert Strong.

Engine #108 being inched back on the rails west of Port Blandford, 1930. The derailment was caused by an ice buildup on the tracks. Despite the locomotive cab being completely demolished, the crew were not seriously injured.

Gertrude Hynes.

#123 at Lethbridge after being re-railed. Engineer Arthur Stanley was seriously injured in the accident and never drove again. Fireman Martin Barnes was also slightly injured, but made a full recovery. It took two weeks to re-rail the locomotive, using jacks, blocking and heavy tackle.

Francis Kelly.

A derailment at Goose Cove, Trinity in the summer of 1942. Passenger cars can be seen on their sides in the foreground, while a work train approaches in the background. Veteran trainman Harold White of Bonavista was killed in this wreck.

An accident involving several gasoline tank cars at Salmon River Bridge. The loaded tank cars were en route to Gander from Lewisporte during World War II. There were an extraordinary number of accidents during the war, mostly attributable to the pressures put on crews and equipment by the war effort.

An unusual collision during the 1950s, involving diesel locomotive #908 and steam locomotive #328. The impact of the crash knocked #328 clear of the tracks, injuring several passengers.

A passenger train being lifted back onto the rails by a heavy wrecking crane, west of Flat Bay in the 1950s.

Burwell Barbour.

A wreck at Gambo Side Hill, 17 May 1951. A pulpwood train from Gambo Pond derailed when a journal on her leading engine broke while she was at speed to make a run at the hill. Engineer Ted Stanley, in the trailing engine #305, was killed and fireman Frank Coles was injured. The tender of #305 lies to the right, while the engine is almost wheels up across the track.

Another view of the wreck a Gambo Side Hill.

Thomas Garrett.

Ted Budden.

Snow fighting on the Gaff Topsails. At left, the steam rotary plow. Chief William O'Reilly stands with his arm outstretched. Right, a modern steel push plow derailed and turned completely around by wet, deep snow. Two 900 class diesel locomotives were also derailed in this accident.

Ted Budden.

A badly snowed-up diesel arrives at Bishop's Falls in the late 1970s. On one occasion I was conductor on a similarly snowed-up train which struck a young girl. Fortunately the snow cushioned the blow and she was uninjured.

I was involved in this rear-end collision at Cooks Brook as conductor of #328, an extra en route from Port aux Basques to Humbermouth. We plowed into another train which had stalled on the main track. #328 was damaged beyond repair, but there were no serious injuries.

Western Star.

Crow Head, 13 September 1966. The author was involved in this head-on collision, which has been called "the worst train disaster in Newfoundland history". Westbound #203 struck eastbound road switcher #920 at 45 mph. Three crewmen of #920 were killed.

BRANCH LINES

*. . .I was to take many trips on the Bonavista
Branch train. . . . The branch line was eighty-eight
miles long and it sometimes took fifteen hours or
more to make the trip, what with all the delays at
stations to load and unload freight. There were also
other delays at intervals along the route while the
train was being watered and sometimes in season
we could get off and pick berries while this was
happening.*

— Jessie Mifflin

Many of the branch lines of the Newfoundland Railway were closed in the 1930s, before my railway career had properly begun. But I have always had fond memories of the branch lines that I knew as a railwayman, particularly the Bonavista branch. From my boyhood in Princeton to my retirement in Brooklyn, the Bonavista branch always played a large role in my life. I spent much of my youth watching the trains on the branch, much of my working life shuttling back and forth between Clarenville and Bonavista, and much of my retirement literally watching the grass grow between the tracks. For all railwaymen the closure of the branch lines to Bonavista, Argentia and Carbonear was a harbinger of the overwhelming sadness that the closure of the main line would bring.

Every collector knows the excitement that springs in his heart when it is discovered that someone has made a major find in the field. Perhaps, then, only fellow collectors will appreciate how glad I am that RCMP Corporal Stephen Parsons decided to take some care in helping clean out the attic of a new home that his friend, Huntley Butler, had purchased in Clarenville. Parsons and Butler found a package of glass negatives dating back to the construction of the Bonavista branch. Corporal Parsons kindly made several of these available to me. They appear throughout this book.

Camps set up for the construction labourers on the Bonavista branch.

The *Fortune* unloading rails for the Bonavista branch at Clarenville in 1909 or 1910. The coastal boat *Argyle* can be seen in the foreground.

The official opening of the Bonavista branch, 8 November 1911. The party on the observation platform at the rear of the private car consists of Lady Morris, Lady Williams, Governor Sir Ralph Williams, Reid Newfoundland Company president William D. Reid and Prime Minister Sir Edward P. Morris.

Provincial Archives of Newfoundland and Labrador.

Provincial Archives of Newfoundland and Labrador.

The Bonavista branch near Trinity. The cribwork at top left was later filled in.

Right: The Bonavista mixed, photographed in 1981, as it passed beneath the Trinity Loop. The Loop was laid out by Reid engineer John P. Powell in 1909, to enable locomotives to cope with the steep grade southwest of Trinity by circling a pond. It remains the only visible train loop in North America.

Below: the opening of the Trinity Loop tourist park.

*John Over, **The Packet**.*

Rosalind Power.

The Bonavista mixed at Princeton station on one of her last runs, in the late summer of 1983. Note the overgrown condition of the roadbed. This station house was my home for 13 years.

Homer Hill.

Inset: trainman T.M. Greening, trainman D.R. Seaward, conductor W.J. Butt and engineer T. Locke.

One of the last runs of the Carbonear mixed, August 1983.

THE WORLD WAR II YEARS

Overworked locomotives that required overhaul, more demand for passenger space than could be found, difficulties of obtaining materials for repairs, train crews dropping with fatigue... these were some of the things which wartime traffic brought to the Newfoundland Railway [which] were taken in their stride by workers in all branches.
— The Story of the Newfoundland Railway in Wartime

The Newfoundland Railway experienced a brief boom during World War II. The railway's life as an important military asset actually began before the war, in the late 1930s with the building of the "Newfoundland Airport" at what is now Gander. Throughout the war years the supplying of Gander was one of the railway's major concerns. The base had to get all its supplies, fuel for the aircraft being ferried across the Atlantic to the war zones of Europe, crushed stone for the runways and coal for its generators through the rail link. Meanwhile civilian traffic increased greatly, as did the number and urgency of pulpwood movements to and from Grand Falls and Corner Brook. For many railwaymen this was the busiest time of their lives. Railway workers and equipment were pushed to the limits of their capacity and beyond.

Like many railwaymen, I would just as soon forget the hardships and tragedies of the war years. However, I have one indelible memory of those years, which perhaps qualifies as the most unusual experience of all my years railroading. I was trainman on a non-scheduled westbound freight that stopped in Gander to pick up empty cars for Bishop's Falls. When we arrived at the airport siding, I was sent by the conductor to check spur lines for empty cars. Unknown to me, some of the spur lines ran quite close to an ammunition dump and oil storage which was quite closely guarded by the Canadian military.

Just as I approached the ammunition dump a squadron of 30 Hudson bombers was landing, so I did not hear the guards' order to halt — or the first few shots that they fired at me. I was eventually held and interrogated for five hours. This not only held up our train (giving me some anxious moments in the process), but also several other trainloads of vital supplies that were waiting for meets with our freight on sidings to the west.

Tom Garrett.

Locomotive #1008 was built by the North British Locomotive Company of Glasgow and was delivered, across the submarine-infested waters of the North Atlantic, in 1941. This engine was renumbered 307 in 1949 and was scrapped in May of 1957.

US Army #500, one of five locomotives provided to the Newfoundland Railway in 1941 under the Lend-Lease Agreement. She was renumbered 1009 by the Newfoundland Railway and became #309 under CN.

Left: one of the tank cars brought to Newfoundland in the war years by the Royal Canadian Air Force, to alleviate shortages at Gander. Right: The #2 passenger train (eastbound), entering Corner Brook yard.

The building of the Newfoundland Airport at Gander. Clockwise from top left: A tractor clearing brush in the early construction stages; dumping crushed stone for the runways; the original railway station; clearing snow from the runways.

106

*Greg Seaward — courtesy **The Gander Beacon**.*

A group of 129 bombers (including B-17s, B-24s and Lancasters) awaiting refueling at Gander.

The railway dock at Lewisporte. Most supplies for Gander were brought to Lewisporte by ship and loaded aboard cars for Gander. Note the fuel storage tanks, top right.

A commemorative poster, produced after the sinking of the *Caribou*.

The German U-boat which sank the *Caribou*. U-69 was built at Kiel in the late 1930s and was under the command of Captain-Lieutenant Ulrich Graf, when she sighted the *Caribou* 40 miles southwest of Channel Head at 2:40 AM on 14 October 1942. U-69 was sunk with all hands by the British cruiser H.M.S. *Viscount* (inset) 17 February 1943.

CN Photo # 46178.

The terminal at Port aux Basques, which assumed great strategic importance during the war years.

A LIFE ON THE RAILWAY

But, the memory of the fastest train in the east will hardly be lost to posterity. Clayton Cook, a retired CN trainman who spends his leisure hours studying steam passenger trains throughout the world, recently researched, planned and formatted a painting of the Overland Limited.
— *Keeping Track*, Summer ,83.

The Newfoundland Railway has given me a lot in the 33 years that I spent, from 1936 to 1940 and from 1941 to 1969, working with trains and railwaymen. If I have any satisfaction in concluding this long-planned book it is because I feel that I served the railway well through my 33 years of work and that, through my union, I also served my co-workers' interests. It is my hope that this book will also provide some small service to generations of Newfoundlanders yet to come.

My father, Leander Cook. After service with the Newfoundland Regiment in France during World War I, Dad returned to a life working on the railway, as a station master at Princeton, Port Union, St. Andrews and Port aux Basques. When I first went to work for the railway I was a maintenance man in the telegraphs department, and I considered following in my father's footsteps through the railway telegraphs department. However, I was so attracted by the romance of the steam locomotives that I had to take a more active role, and became a trainman and conductor.

St. Andrew's station. My father walks in front of the station house and my sisters Phyllis and Lenora stand in the doorway. At one time during my father's tenure at St. Andrew's the wind speed was measured at 127 mph, before the wind gauge was blown off the building!
Inset: my brother, Sidney Cook, also a trainman for many years.

I worked briefly at Argentia in 1940, before returning to the railway in 1941. This photograph was taken shortly after my return, at the site of a derailment at Lethbridge. Standing on the running board of the locomotive are Harold Thompson, Augustus Miles, the author, and an unknown sectionman.

A passenger train crew, photographed in the early 1950s. The author, the conductor, stands at left. The trainmen are John O'Reilly and Kevin Dwyer. This was a special train put on for a visit by the Governor-General of Canada.

NEWFOUNDLAND RAILWAY
THE OVERLAND ROUTE

Ready and anxious to serve your ❧ ❧ ❧ ❧ every Transportation Requirement.

Ship and Travel "Overland" for Service Unexcelled.

An advertisement for the "Overland" from 1943.

*John Over, **The Packet***.

One of the things that I am proudest of is the success that met my campaign to save the Trinity Loop once I heard that the rails were going to be torn up on the Bonavista branch. In recognition of my efforts, businessman Francis Kelly did me the honour of naming his tourist attraction the Clayton Cook Loop Railway. L-R: the author, park owner Kelly and Trinity mayor Dr. Phyllis Duncan.

The visit of Canadian National president Donald Gordon, during the early 1950s. Top, L-R: the author, L. Glavine. Middle, L-R: H. Grayson, W. Fitzpatrick. Bottom, L-R: C. Puddister, Mr. Atkinson, E. Alexander, D. Dingwell, L. Stevenson, D. Gordon, V. McCarthy, R. Vaughn.
Inset: my conductor's certificate.

THE END OF THE LINE

At the date of Union, or as soon thereafter as practicable, Canada will take over the following services and will as from the date of Union relieve the Province of Newfoundland of the public costs incurred in respect of each service taken over, namely, (a) the Newfoundland Railway. . .
— Term 31 of the Terms of Union.

The end of the war found the Newfoundland Railway's equipment (and personnel) in badly run-down condition. After Confederation the system was absorbed by Canadian National and wages, safety and working conditions were considerably improved. New locomotives and rolling stock were added to the system and the conversion from coal- to oil-fired locomotives was completed. There were some difficulties for railwaymen in absorbing the new rules on a system that the Newfoundlanders considered that they knew better than anyone else, but for the most part the transition was a smooth one.

In 1952 the system began another transition. Dieselization really picked up in 1956 and was virtually completed by the end of 1957.

In 1969 came the end of the trans-island passenger service, which was replaced by roadcruiser buses. Containerization also became the order of the day for much freight. It was also in 1969

that I took early retirement.

In 1979, Terra Transport became a separate entity. By the 1980s the writing was on the wall that the train would soon be abandoned all together. The Bonavista branch was closed down in 1983, followed by Argentia and Carbonear the next year. Then, in 1988, the federal and provincial governments reached an agreement to close down the main line.

As a retired railwayman I was saddened by the railway's progressive demise, but I am willing to suppose that the company and the province had no other choice. In the years to come, as the Newfoundland railwaymen pass to their reward, I sincerely hope that the Newfoundland Railway will not ever be truly gone. I pray that the railway will always remain a part of our memory as a people, as it was a vital part of our culture for more than 100 years.

1948. Engineer Arch McLellan is handed a copy of the *Western Star*. The headline reads "Close Race in Referendum Vote — Confederation 78,823; Responsible Government 71,334". The locomotive is #1013, built for the US Army and provided to the Newfoundland Railway under lend-lease. This engine would soon be renumbered 313, once CN took over the system. It was scrapped in 1957.

CN Photo # 46343.

121

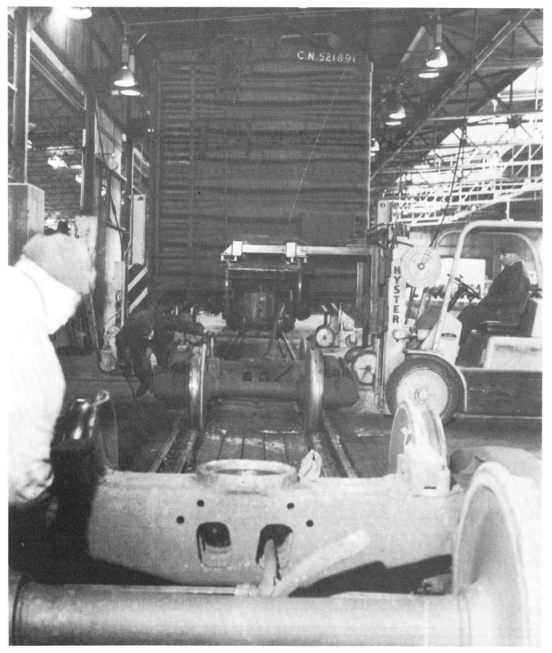

The truck-to-truck transfer shed at Port aux Basques. Standard gauge trucks are being removed from boxcars, to be replaced by narrow gauge trucks.

CN Photo # 70143-23.

The Gambo-Clarenville train-car ferry, in use before the completion of the Trans-Canada Highway in 1965.

Montreal, 1956. The MV *Christian Smith* loads diesel locomotives for the Newfoundland Railway.

Terra Transport.

A roadcruiser bus and container truck alongside a diesel locomotive.

Evening Telegram.

Corner Brook, 2 July 1969. Crowds gather to see off the last eastbound passenger train.

Homer Hill.

The Carbonear mixed approaches a dilapidated Avondale Station in 1983. Inset: the crew for the last run. Trainman Job Blackmore, engineer Gerry Maddigan, trainman Tom Carew, conductor Gord Smith and trainman Jerry McGinnis.

Richard Forest.

The last Argentia mixed train as it prepares to depart St. John's, 19 September 1984.
Inset: the crew for the last run — engineer Gerry Maddigan, trainman Wilson Butt, conductor Gord Smith and trainman Paul Murphy.

The last railway timetable, which expired 30 September 1988.

TERRATRANSPORT
TIME TABLE

106

EFFECTIVE SUNDAY, MAY 1st, 1988
REFER TO PAGE 1 FOR EFFECTIVE TIME, AND FOR
OTHER TIME AND DATE CHANGES THAT WILL OCCUR

SAFETY IS OF THE FIRST IMPORTANCE
IN THE DISCHARGE OF DUTY

J.H. EASTON
PRESIDENT AND GENERAL MANAGER
ST. JOHN'S

R.J. WALSH
SUPT. TRANSPORTATION
ST. JOHN'S

Terra Transport.

The last train operating in the province. 59 km of the 420 km Quebec North Shore and Labrador Railway is across our province's territory. This 260-car ore train is headed by three GM model SD-40 turbocharged diesels. Two more remote-controlled diesels are at two thirds the length of the train.

Quebec North Shore and Labrador Railway.

The last scheduled train westbound to Corner Brook 30 Sept 1988. Photographed at Bishop's Falls overpass.

Inset: trainmen Gerald Turner, Patrick O'Reilly and William Penney. Engineer Patrick O'Reilly and conductor Carl Dillon stand at front.

C. Hoddinott.

Workmen lifting the first rail at mileage 340 in the Gaff Topsails 12 October 1988.

The end of the line. Dismantling the track in the Gaff Topsails area. Workmen pictured are Isaac Wall, Robert Hynes, Lorne Simmonds and Hubert Hollett.